DEDICATION

To my lovely granddaughter, Chloe Lanae' Coleman. You leave sparkle everywhere you go. You remind me so much of your mother growing up. You are truly her carbon copy. I love all that you are and all that you are yet to become, as you grow into a godly woman of integrity.

I pray that you have the courage to follow your dreams. You are beautiful, adventurous, talented and very intelligent, and I dedicate this book to you, my darling.

Many desire to have an impact on the world. You, sweetheart, have already begun to make a difference. The works of your hands and the works of your mouth will always have power. I pray that the Lord will continue to bless you and all those connected to you. Continue to grow in grace, as you walk into your redemptive purpose.

Love to you from your Abuelita Jackie

LEARNING TO USE YOUR GREATEST WEAPON

McDougal & Associates

Servants of Christ and Stewards of the
Mysteries of God

LEARNING TO USE YOUR GREATEST WEAPON

by

Prophetess Jackie Harewood

Published by:

McDougal & Associates
18896 Greenwell Springs RD
Greenwell Springs, LA 70739
www.thepublishedword.com

McDougal & Associates is dedicated to the spreading of the Gospel of Jesus Christ to as many people as possible in the shortest time possible.

ISBN 978-1-940461-56-4

Printed in the US, the UK and Australia
For Worldwide Distribution

ACKNOWLEDGEMENTS

I must acknowledge my God, who has allowed me to have the experiences that have aligned me with spiritual warfare. His Holy Spirit has trained me and taught me the craft of war.

For the word of God is living and active, and sharper than any two-edged sword, penetrating even as far as the division of soul and spirit, and of joints and marrows, and able to judge the thoughts and intentions of the heart.

Hebrews 4:12, BSB

CONTENTS

INTRODUCTION

Those who have read my book, *Ballistic Apostolic Prayer*, now realize that there is so much more to intercessory prayer and spiritual warfare than we have imagined. In this book, I will continue to uncover the secrets of praying with power, praying with wisdom, praying by the Spirit, praying prayers that are specifically targeted and, therefore, can be much more effective.

For too long now, our prayers have been very generalized. It is time to focus on the right targets and to use the right kind of weapons and the right kind of ammunition. It is time you concentrate on *Learning to Use Your Most Powerful Weapon.*

Prophetess Jackie Harewood
Baton Rouge, Louisiana

CHAPTER 1

UNDERSTAND THE LEVELS OF SPIRITUAL WARFARE

For we wrestle not against flesh and blood, but against principalities, against powers, against the rulers of the darkness of this world, against spiritual wickedness in high places. Ephesians 6:12

This is not a wrestling match against a human opponent. We are wrestling with rulers, authorities, the powers who govern this world of darkness, and spiritual forces that control evil in the heavenly world.

GW

A Personal Level of Spiritual Warfare (Principalities)

This speaks of demons afflicting an individual. This struggle mainly happens in the lives of individual lives and is mainly to do with personal decisions and choices between good and evil. Attacks in this level mainly come in the form of temptations:

We know that the Law is spiritual. But I am merely a human, and I have been sold as a slave to sin. In fact, I don't understand why I act the way I do. I don't do what I know is right. I do the things I hate.

Although I don't do what I know is right, I agree that the Law is good.
                    Romans 7:14-16, CEV

Pray that you will not fall into temptation:

Watch ye and pray, lest ye enter into temptation. The spirit truly is ready, but the flesh is weak. Mark 14:38

Ground Level Spiritual Warfare (Powers)

This refers to the outward man-ifestation of demonic powers or activity and demon oppression and mainly includes spirits of infirmity, deaf and dumb spirits, spirits of lust, blaspheming against God, the spirit of intellect, etc.

Jesus set a woman free from a spirit of infirmity:

And, behold, there was a woman which had a spirit of infirmity eighteen years, and was bowed together, and could in no wise lift up herself. And when Jesus saw her, he called her to him, and said unto her, Woman, thou art loosed from thine infirmity. And he laid his hands on her: and immediately she was made straight, and glorified God.

Luke 13:11-13

A deaf and dumb spirit required prayer and fasting to defeat:

And one of the multitude answered and said, Master, I have brought unto thee my son, which hath a dumb spirit; and wheresoever he taketh him, he teareth him: and he foameth, and gnasheth with his teeth, and pineth away: and I spake to thy disciples that they should cast him out; and they could not.

Mark 9:17-18

And he said unto them, This kind can come forth by nothing, but by prayer and fasting. Mark 9:29

Occult Level of Spiritual Warfare (Rulers of the Darkness of this World)

This refers to warfare with human spirits, human systems, and powers. It is warfare against the organized forces of darkness, such as witchcraft,

Freemasonry, cults, superstitions rituals, Satanism, mediums, spiritists, fortune telling, palmistry, astrology, horoscopes, idolatry, etc.

Paul and Silas cast out a spirit of divination:

> *One day when we were going to the place of prayer, a female servant met us. She was possessed by an evil spirit that told fortunes. She made a lot of money for her owners by telling fortunes.*   Acts 16:16, GW

Strategic Level Spiritual Warfare: Territorial Level Spiritual Warfare (Spiritual Wickedness in High Places)

These are known in the God's Word translation as *"spiritual forces that control evil in the heavenly world.*" This level is sometimes referred to as the "territorial" level. This refers to spiritual strongholds that keep a certain area, city, province or state, community, nation or nations under control:

> *For our wrestling is not against flesh and blood, but against the principalities [rulers], against the powers [authorities], against the world-rulers of this darkness, against the spiritual hosts of wickedness in the heavenly places.*
>
> Ephesians 6:12, ASV

It is important to remember that we are not fighting against flesh and blood, but against spiritual forces, demonic spirits that rule in the heavenly places.

Principalities and Rulers: The word *principalities* itself means "an area or state that is being ruled by a prince," so this demonic level of hierarchy has a larger influence and dominion. It means that it has a larger region, territory, nation or nations that it influences with its demonic works.

We must understand the different levels of spiritual warfare, the demonic hierarchy or demonic influence the devil has planned, and how he functions and makes war. Depending upon the place, the principalities that rule over villages, towns, cities, regions, or countries may differ. Controlling geographical areas, nations, villages, towns, cities, or countries is a principle strategy of the enemy.

Historically, one of the principalities that ruled over the southern states of our country and over other areas of the world was slavery. In some areas, some cities are said to be ruled by violence and drugs. The blood of Jesus Christ, the Word of God, praise and worship, the name of Jesus Christ, prayers and intercessions, and many more weapons are all a part of the arsenal we have for spiritual warfare. Even anointed preaching and teaching are a part of our powerful warfare against the dark forces in the heavenly places:

> *Then Jesus came to them and said, "All authority in heaven and on earth has been given to me."*
> Matthew 28:18, NIV

Jesus' intent was this:

THE MANIFOLD WISDOM OF GOD might now be made known through the church to the rulers and the authorities in the heavenly places. This was in accordance with the eternal purpose which He carried out in Christ Jesus our Lord. Ephesians 3:10-11, NASB
Emphasis added

For the word of God is quick, and powerful, and sharper than any twoedged sword, piercing even to the dividing asunder of soul and spirit, and of the joints and marrow, and is a discerner of the thoughts and intents of the heart. Hebrews 4:12

We must now put His intent into action, bringing the will of Heaven to Earth. Learn to understand the levels of spiritual warfare.

Chapter 2

LEARNING TO USE YOUR GREATEST WEAPON

For I will give you a mouth and wisdom, which all your adversaries shall not be able to gainsay nor resist. Luke 21:15

In the Old Testament, the power was in the feet, but in the New Testament, the power is in your mouth. Your mouth is the weapon of the twenty-first century.

In the old paradigm, when trying to acquire something, such a property, you marched around it seven times. Joshua was an example:

By faith the walls of Jericho fell down, after they were compassed about seven days. Hebrews 11:30

This was the promise given to Moses and then to Joshua:

Every place that the sole of your foot shall tread upon, that have I given unto you, as I said unto Moses.
Joshua 1:3

One day in 1994 God spoke to my husband that He was going to give Faith City a permanent home. We had been meeting in a hotel ballroom for more than a year. My husband was then led to the exact location, which was an old lumber company.

Next God gave my husband the strategy of Joshua 1:3. Early one morning (at 3:00 a.m.), he woke me to say that God had given him instructions to go walk on the property. I responded to that immediately, and we dressed and went to walk around the whole block seven times. After completing our walk, we were confident that God had sealed the deal.

We knew something had broken in the Spirit because there was a physical reaction to our spiritual action. Our prophetic act caused such a disturbance in the spirit world that an emergency vehicle had to be called for someone who lived on the route we had walked. Later we learned that the person taken to the hospital was in the key house on that block, a place where the community congregated to practice ungodly activity. God was giving us the land.

Today there is a paradigm shift. The victory is no longer just in our feet. It is now in our mouth. It's in a *now* word from God spoken through our mouth.

We possess with our mouth:

> *For I will give you a mouth and wisdom, which all your adversaries shall not be able to gainsay nor resist.* Luke 21:15

Mouth is the Hebrew word, *stom'-a,* which denotes "the front or edge of a weapon." Every time you release an anointed word from your mouth, you are wielding a dangerous weapon, to pierce the darkness. With this weapon, you can destroy external enemies such as poverty, failure, cancer, diabetes, HIV, and the like. You can also destroy internal enemies such as fear, anxiety, doubt, bipolarism, betrayism, disappointism, and other *isms* that plague our nature.

We use our mouth as the front edge of God's sword to decree a thing:

Thou shalt also decree a thing, and it shall be established unto thee: and the light shall shine upon thy ways. Job 22:28

This word *decree* or *gaw-zar'*, comes from a Hebrew word that denotes "to cut down or cut off, to destroy, divide":

For the word of God is quick, and powerful, and sharper than any twoedged sword, piercing even to the dividing asunder of soul and spirit, and of the joints and marrow, and is a discerner of the thoughts and intents of the heart.

Hebrews 4:12

Decree is an action word that, when launched out of your mouth, has every intention to cut down, cut off and destroy every tactic of the enemy. A decree divides and conquers.

A decree, when applied with the anointing, denies access to Satan and sets up a barrier to restrict him and his cohorts from a certain place, a group, or a situation. He is prohibited from exercising any privilege and under orders from the Holy Spirit to cease and desist.

The thing we decree is the revealed proceeding word from God that shall be established. This word *establish* is *koom* in the Hebrew, which denotes, "to rise, to rise up against, to get up, to stand up, to stir up, to strengthen, and to succeed." If we speak it with the precision and accuracy of the Spirit of God, we will accomplish the design of our destiny.

A decree actually influences our mind, inspiring us to rise up and resist the forces that restrain us. Our spirit is then stirred up and strengthened to succeed.

A prophetic decree may be in the form of an announcement, a declaration or a command, but it must be made in faith, causing the impossible to happen. Some examples are:

The announcement of Mary's pregnancy:

And, behold, thou shalt conceive in thy womb, and bring forth a son, and shalt call his name Jesus.

Luke 1:31

The announcement of Jesus' birth:

And the angel said unto them, Fear not: for, behold, I bring you good tidings of great joy, which shall be to all people. For unto you is born this day in the city of David a Saviour, which is Christ the Lord. And this shall be a sign unto you; Ye shall find the babe wrapped in swaddling clothes, lying in a manger.

Luke 2:10-12

The announcement that Jesus was alive:

And when they found not his body, they came, saying, that they had also seen a vision of angels, which said that he was alive.

Luke 24:23

The announcement of Jesus' return:

Which also said, Ye men of Galilee, why stand ye gazing up into heaven?

this same Jesus, which is taken up from you into heaven, shall so come in like manner as ye have seen him go into heaven. Acts 1:11

The announcement that Zechariah and Elizabeth would bear a son:

The angel said to him, "Do not be afraid, Zacharias, for your petition has been heard, and your wife Elizabeth will bear you a son, and you will give him the name John.
Luke 1:13, NASB

The announcement made at the baptism of Jesus:

And lo a voice from heaven, saying, This is my beloved Son, in whom I am well pleased. Matthew 3:17

Angels announced the glad tidings during that time frame. They can still make announcements, but today God has empowered believers to make announcements of His intentions in the Earth realm. You can announce to Heaven your God-given, redemptive plan and then pursue it with great expectation. The future is yours to command, as you learn to use your greatest weapon.

CHAPTER 3

USING ANOINTED WORD PROJECTILES

For the word of God is quick, and powerful, and sharper than any twoedged sword, piercing even to the dividing asunder of soul and spirit, and of the joints and marrow, and is a discerner of the thoughts and intents of the heart.

Hebrews 4:12

Speaking anointed word projectiles is an excellent way to intercede for others and alter their destiny. This word *projectile* is defined as "something such as a bullet or rocket that is shot from a weapon." In the spiritual realm, we do not use physical bullets nor rockets. Rather, we use God's will, defined by His Word.

"Something thrown as a weapon." God's Word released into the atmosphere is our weapon, propelled with force through the air by the movement of our voice.

"A body projected by external force and continuing in motion by its own inertia, by the law of gravity, especially a missile for a weapon such as a firearm." In the spiritual realm, the body projected is governed by spiritual forces and continues in motion, not by the

Law of Gravity, but by the Law of the
Spirit of Life in Christ Jesus:

> *For the law of the Spirit of life in
> Christ Jesus hath made me free
> from the law of sin and death.*
> Romans 8:2

"A self-propelling weapon, as a
rocket." In the spiritual realm, the self-
propelling weapon is the Word, the
promises of God, prophecy, a God-
inspired dream, and/or a vision God
has given an individual:

> *For the word of God is quick, and
> powerful, and sharper than any
> twoedged sword, piercing even to
> the dividing asunder of soul and
> spirit, and of the joints and marrow,*

and is a discerner of the thoughts and intents of the heart.

Hebrews 4:12

Is not my word like as a fire? saith the LORD; and like a hammer that breaketh the rock in pieces?

Jeremiah 23:29

All scripture is given by inspiration of God, and is profitable for doctrine, for reproof, for correction, for instruction in righteousness.

2 Timothy 3:16

Our word projectiles serve to obtain both strength and support for us from God. Anointed prophetic words spoken supply us with motives for endurance. They supply the confidence and hope we need to succeed:

This charge I commit unto thee, son Timothy, according to the prophecies which went before on thee, that thou by them mightest war a good warfare. 1 Timothy 1:18

The phrase *"mightiest war"* in the Greek denotes "to serve in a military campaign with its strenuous duties and activities." It also indicates "to contend with carnal inclinations."

"Good warfare" denotes "morally good, virtuous, honest, worthy." It is a military service, a valuable apostolic career, as "on with hardship and danger."

Our anointed prophetic words are also among the defensive weapons God has provided for us to use. These anointed word projectiles have great influence in the lives of those around us. Spoken anointed word projectiles can bring hope, encouragement, and direction to our families, friends, and others.

A spoken anointed word projectile is a positive, biblical statement that invokes the blessing of God in the life of another. This word *invoke* is defined by Merriam-Webster.com as "to mention something in an attempt to make people feel a certain way or have a certain idea in their mind." Spiritual encouragement will activate, motivate and inspire the recipient to gravitate toward the greatness God has planned for them. He said:

For I know the thoughts that I think toward you, saith the LORD, thoughts of peace, and not of evil, to give you an expected end.

Jeremiah 29:11

When you speak anointed word projectiles, they confirm God's will in the Earth realm. You are declaring the purpose of the Lord:

The counsel of the LORD standeth for ever, the thoughts of his heart to all generations. Psalm 33:11

This word *standeth* is the Hebrew word *aw-mad* that denotes "abide, continue, be employed, endure, establish, and tarry." Your anointed word projectiles encircle the individual they are sent to, continue without fading or being lost, and remain in existence, setting up the necessary conditions to guide the recipient. What you have placed in motion becomes committed to seeing God's will manifested.

James wrote:

Confess your faults one to another, and pray one for another, that ye may be healed. The effectual fervent prayer of a righteous man availeth much.   James 5:16

This phrase *effectual fervent* is the Greek word *energeo*, which denotes "to be active, efficient and work effectually in." You can see how your anointed word projectiles carry out their assignment. When you send them out on assignment, they become active, achieving maximum productivity with minimum wasted effort or expense on your part. They are assigned to a target, and they fulfill their mission.

"To refer to (something) in support of your ideas":

Submit to God, and you will have peace;
then things will go well for you.

Job 22:21, NLT

Locating the scriptures, introducing the ideas of the mind of God, and then releasing that declaration into the atmosphere will propel the individual into the path God has designed for them. Every individual has a free will, and therefore this does not force them to conform to the will of God. Rather, it give them a clear path to make correct choices.

There is always an issue to consider, which is heavy interference from Satan and the flesh:

In whom the god of this world hath blinded the minds of them which believe not, lest the light of the glorious gospel of Christ, who is the image of God, should shine unto them.
2 Corinthians 4:4

To insure that the individual's mind is free from blinders, it is necessary to use binding and loosing, to get the individual in an unopposed frame of mind to make a decision. In two instances, the New Testament refers to this strategy:

And I will give unto thee the keys of the kingdom of heaven: and whatsoever thou shalt bind on earth shall be bound in heaven: and whatsoever thou shalt loose on earth shall be loosed in heaven.

Matthew 16:19

Verily I say unto you, Whatsoever ye shall bind on earth shall be bound in heaven: and whatsoever ye shall loose on earth shall be loosed in heaven. Matthew 18:18

We bind the forces of Satan in Jesus' name and command the blinders to be removed. Command the light of the glorious Gospel to enlighten their decision-making processes, in Jesus' name.

"To make use of a law or a right." Spiritually, God's authoritative Word governs and has the final say in any matter.

For as the rain cometh down, and the snow from heaven, and returneth not thither, but watereth the earth, and maketh it bring forth and bud, that it may give seed to the sower, and bread to the eater: so shall my word be that goeth forth out of my mouth: it shall not return unto me void, but it shall accomplish that which I please, and it shall prosper in the thing whereto I sent it. Isaiah 55:10-11

"To petition for help or support." You enlist angels to legislate and negotiate as needed, to prepare the atmosphere for the breakthrough.

"To appeal to or cite as authority." According to Merriam-Webster.com, the definition of *appeal,* as it applies to law, is "a legal proceeding by which a case is brought before a higher court for review of the decision of a lower court." When you release the proper will of God, you are defying the lower court of Earth-bound plans of the opposition, and you are presenting solid evidence of the confirmed will and plan for God's redemptive destiny to manifest. You take the initiative to call forth the approved, agreed plan of creation, and you call into effect the expedition to the destiny.

The power of spoken anointed word projectiles comes from God. He Himself has blessed us:

Blessed be the God and Father of our Lord Jesus Christ, who hath blessed us with all spiritual blessings in heavenly places in Christ.

Ephesians 1:3

"To invoke a benediction upon." *Benediction* is defined as "a ceremonial prayer invoking divine protection."

A BLESSING IS AN INSTRUMENT OF GOD'S LOVE

Our words have presence, power, potential and prophetic implication. They have legal presence to do good or to do harm. The Bible describes the potential impact of our words in verses such as these:

48

Death and life are in the power of the tongue: and they that love it shall eat the fruit thereof.

Proverbs 18:21

Pleasant words are as an honeycomb, sweet to the soul, and health to the bones. Proverbs 16:24

Heaviness in the heart of man maketh it stoop: but a good word maketh it glad. Proverbs 12:25

In the New Testament, the English word *bless* is a translation of the Greek word *eulogeo*. According to *Strong's*, *eulogeo* means "to speak well of, or invoke a benediction upon, and prosper." When you bless others, you direct God's goodness to them; you intercede

49

for them, you speak well of them, and you stand in the gap for them, as you come boldly to the throne of grace in faith:

And I sought for a man among them that should make up the hedge, and stand in the gap before me for the land, that I should not destroy it: but I found none.
Ezekiel 22:30

Let us therefore come boldly unto the throne of grace that we may obtain mercy, and find grace to help in time of need. Hebrews 4:16

For your anointed word projectile, try using the biblical structure of Numbers 6:24-26. The priestly blessing recorded in this verse provides us with an excellent example of a godly blessing:

The LORD bless thee, and keep thee:
The LORD make his face shine upon thee, and be gracious unto thee:
The LORD lift up his countenance upon thee, and give thee peace.

Numbers 6:24-26

The Lord bless you, and keep you [protect you, sustain you, and guard you];
The Lord make His face shine upon you [with favor], and be gracious to you [surrounding you with lovingkindness];
The Lord lift up His countenance (face) upon you [with divine

approval] and give you peace [a tranquil heart and life].
                    Numbers 6:24-26, AMP

You can use this blessing as a framework for composing your own blessings. It can be helpful to look up the meanings of key words in these verses. A complete detailed knowledge of these words will expand your understanding of the message and equip you to apply its truths more effectively.

USE DISCERNMENT TO INTERVENE EFFECTIVELY

It takes time and effort to search out appropriate anointed word projectiles. Ask the Lord to make you attentive to His Spirit as you read the Scriptures, discerning which words, phrases, and concepts He wants you to share on behalf of another.

Discerning is defined by Merriam-Webster.com as "to be able to see and understand people, things, or situations clearly and intelligently and showing insight and understanding." Through discerning, the Holy Spirit will assist you in affirming God's will by revealing to you what you can pronounce in your anointed word projectile:

Howbeit when he, the Spirit of truth, is come, he will guide you into all truth: for he shall not speak of himself; but whatsoever he shall hear, that shall he speak: and he will shew you things to come. John 16:13

CRAFTING YOUR ANOINTED WORD PROJECTILE

When God puts a desire in your heart to bless someone, be attentive to the needs that person may have. With that person in mind, you can ask the questions below to help you discern the kind of intervention projectile that person needs. Consider using the related scripture references for crafting your anointed word projectile:

- Is the fruit of the Spirit evident in this person's life (see Galatians 5:22-25)?
- Is this person serving others in love (see Galatians 5:13 and Luke 6:27-38)?
- Is this person seeking God's guidance so that they can carry

out the good works God has prepared for them to do (see James 3:12-13, 1 Timothy 6:11-19, Titus 3:8 and Hebrews 10:24)?

- Is this person submitting to his or her God-ordained authorities (see Hebrews 13:17, James 4:7, Colossians 3:18, and 1 Peter 2:13-14)?

- Does it appear that something may be competing with this person's devotion to God? (see Matthew 6:33)?

- Are there particular temptations that seem to present big challenges in this person's life (see Matthew 6:13, 1 Corinthians 10:13, Matthew 26:41, 1 Timothy 6:9-12, and Luke 8:4-18)?

- Are you aware of any fears, hurts, or pressures that this person is facing (see Galatians 6:1-3, James 5:16, Romans 12:1-15, and Ephesians 4:32)?

As you consider these questions, God can reveal to you areas of need in the person's life. Then ask the Holy Spirit to guide you to specific verses or passages of scripture that can be used as anointed word projectiles related to their need.

Learn to use anointed word projectiles.

CHAPTER 4

INCREASING YOUR PROPHETIC AUTHORITY

The people that do know their God shall be strong, and do exploits.

Daniel 11:32

PROPHETIC AUTHORITY AND THE MINISTRY OF ELISHA

A group of prophets were building a larger meeting place. As one of them cut down a tree, the iron ax head he was using fell into the water and sank out of sight. In distress, because the ax head was borrowed, he called on

Elisha to help him find it (see 2 Kings 6:1-6).

PROPHETIC AUTHORITY

Here we have an entire company of prophets, and yet when a situation occurred that required a miracle, only one prophet, Elisha, known as "the man of God," had the authority to overcome the laws of nature and cause the iron ax head to float.

A similar thing took place in 2 Kings 4:38-41 during a gathering of the prophets. This time there was a crisis in the kitchen, and they were faced with poison stew. Again, among the entire group of prophets, it was only Elisha who had the spiritual authority to cause a miracle to take place.

Will you be one of the many, or one of the few? Many can bring prophetic encouragement, but only a few have yieldedness to be used to bring forth miracles and breakthroughs. Only a few can cause a miracle to take place by the word of their mouth or through a prophetic act.

KEYS TO INCREASING YOUR PROPHETIC AUTHORITY

If you are called to prophetic ministry or a prophetic office, this scenario will be most applicable to you. I believe God is calling all of us who have a prophetic gift to grow further in the anointing He has for us.

Wherever we go in our daily lives, there are people who need a breakthrough miracle, and Jesus is inviting us to partner with Him in His Kingdom authority. With that in mind, following are five keys from the life of Elisha on how to grow in your prophetic authority:

1. Know God through Intimate Relationship and Know His Word.

Among the prophets, Elisha was known for both his intimacy and authority:

> *The people that do know their God shall be strong, and do exploits.*
> Daniel 11:32

Develop your personal intimate relationship with God. This includes knowing Him through His Word, having a comprehensive knowledge of the Bible and standing by its authority without compromise.

2. Find Someone to Serve.

Elisha spent years serving as Elijah's attendant. Some of the tasks he was required to do during this apprenticeship were menial, yet significant:

> *But Jehoshaphat said, Is there not here a prophet of the* Lord, *that we may enquire of the* Lord *by him? And one of the king of Israel's servants answered and said, Here is Elisha the son of Shaphat, which poured water on the hands of Elijah.*   2 Kings 3:11

During his time of serving, Elisha was observing, learning and being infused with the faith and spiritual authority that was on Elijah's life.

Start where God has placed you. Your Elijah does not have to be a prophet. It may be just serving in your local church. Be faithful and let God move you forward in your gift. If you are a ministry leader or senior pastor, find a godly apostolic leader to relate to.

3. Step Out of Your Comfort Zone.

Elisha went further than other prophets of his time in his quest to follow God's call on his life. He pursued Elijah diligently, not knowing when, but knowing that God was calling his master to Heaven. A group of fifty prophets stopped at Jericho, while Elisha pursued Elijah past the point of no return.

The waters of the Jordan miraculously parted for Elijah, and Elisha followed. He knew that his destiny was on the horizon:

> *And Elijah said unto him, Tarry, I pray thee, here; for the LORD hath sent me to Jordan. And he said, As the LORD liveth, and as thy soul liveth, I will not leave thee. And they two went on.*   2 Kings 2:6

The increased prophetic authority that God has for you is beyond the comfort zone of your history and past experience. Your blessing is in the pressing.

4. Learn How to Release the Power of God.

Elisha understood his God-given authority and was able to release the power of God into situations through a bold word or prophetic act, as the Holy Spirit led him. By the same example, we need to understand that we have stewardship of God's power.

Learn the dynamics between the prophetic *now* word of God and releasing His power. Speak life-giving words, and expect those anointed words to shift atmospheres and circumstances.

5. Be Willing to Empower Others on the Journey.

In the text of 2 Kings 6, Elisha was leading a company of prophets. This was a training ground and a demonstration to them. Our gifts, talents and abilities will lay dormant until they are awakened by one more experienced than ourselves. Be that someone for another believer.

Elisha was not holding his knowledge to himself. He demonstrated to others what could be possible. He gave of his time and resources to bring up the next prophetic generation. The prophetic gift, along with the wisdom and faith of its operation, is not for us to hold on to. It is not an exclusive gift or ministry. It is from the Lord and should be used for His glory and the building of His Kingdom.

Like Elijah and Elisha before us, be willing to encourage and empower others in their gifts and ministries, and your fruitfulness will be multiplied many times over.

Learn to increase your prophetic anointing.

CHAPTER 5

EMPLOYING PROPHETIC PRAYER

Wherefore he is able also to save them to the uttermost that come unto God by him, seeing he ever liveth to make intercession for them. Hebrews 7:25

E.M. Bounds asserted, "Without prayer, nothing happens!" So, what happens when the prophet prays? Prophetic prayer invites the intercession of the Son to the Father. Jesus commanded us to pray for God's will in Heaven to be done here on Earth:

After this manner therefore pray ye: Our Father which art in heaven, Hallowed be thy name. Thy kingdom come. Thy will be done in earth, as it is in heaven.

Matthew 6:9-10

Jesus, our High Priest at the throne of God, is praying God's will for the saints continually, and we should too.

We have been reaching awkwardly and trying to pull down the Kingdom of God as a prophetic act. But the motion of reaching up to pull down the Kingdom of God is not accurate when you pray with a ballistic anointing. The Kingdom of God is within us.

Therefore, when we pray *"thy kingdom, come thy will be done, on earth as it is in heaven,"* we must remember that the Kingdom of God is not upward. Rather, the Kingdom of God is inward:

Neither shall they say, Lo here! or, lo there! for, behold, the kingdom of God is within you. Luke 17:21

As we place a demand on the Word and operate from the faith realm of relying on the presence of the Kingdom with all power and influence of all heavenly resources to accomplish our task, we enter into the faith realm of ballistic apostolic prayer and are elevated to a dimension equivalent to extraordinary authority. We hear God's words and speak them in prayer.

We have the grace to birth the invisible into the visible and the impossible into the possible:

And Jesus looking upon them saith, With men it is impossible, but not with God: for with God all things are possible. Mark 10:27

For God, who commanded the light to shine out of darkness, hath shined in our hearts, to give the light of the knowledge of the glory of God in the face of Jesus Christ. But we have this treasure in earthen vessels, that the excellency of the power may be of God, and not of us. 2 Corinthians 4:6-7

Prophetic intercession is biblical. From several biblical records, we can get an idea of the proper formula to use:

Now Jericho was straitly shut up because of the children of Israel: none went out, and none came in. And the LORD said unto Joshua, See, I have given into thine hand Jericho, and the king thereof, and the mighty men of valour. And ye shall compass the city, all ye men of war, and go round about the city once. Thus shalt thou do six days. And seven priests shall bear before the ark seven trumpets of rams' horns: and the seventh day ye shall compass the city seven times, and the priests shall blow with the trumpets. And it shall come to pass, that when they make a long blast with the ram's horn, and when ye hear the sound of the trumpet, all the people shall shout with a great shout; and the wall of the city shall fall down flat, and the people shall ascend up every man straight before him. Joshua 6:1-5

Thou also, son of man, take thee a tile, and lay it before thee, and pourtray upon it the city, even Jerusalem: And lay siege against it, and build a fort against it, and cast a mount against it; set the camp also against it, and set battering rams against it round about. Moreover take thou unto thee an iron pan, and set it for a wall of iron between thee and the city: and set thy face against it, and it shall be besieged, and thou shalt lay siege against it. This shall be a sign to the house of Israel.

Lie thou also upon thy left side, and lay the iniquity of the house of Israel upon it: according to the number of the days that thou shalt lie upon it thou shalt bear their iniquity. For I have laid upon thee the years of their iniquity, according to the number of the days, three hundred and ninety days: so shalt thou bear the iniquity of the house of Israel. And when thou hast accomplished them, lie again on thy right side, and thou shalt bear the iniquity of the house of Judah forty days: I have appointed thee each day for a year. Therefore thou shalt set thy face toward the siege of Jerusalem, and thine arm shall be uncovered, and thou shalt prophesy against it. And, behold, I will lay bands upon thee, and thou shalt not turn thee from one side to another, till thou hast ended the days of thy siege.

Ezekiel 4:1-8

This is by no means the extent of the examples found in the Word of God. I encourage you to study more biblical examples to enhance your understanding of this topic.

In prophetic intercession, we intercede according to the will and leading of the Holy Spirit. Although the Lord is sovereign, He desires to partner with us to accomplish His will and purpose for our lives and those of others.

Learn to employ prophetic prayer.

CHAPTER 6

PERSONALIZING AN ANOINTED WORD PROJECTILE

For God hath not given us the spirit of fear; but of power, and of love, and of a sound mind [discipline, self-control]. 2 Timothy 1:7

Your friend struggles with fear and anxiety. You could use a concordance, when necessary, to look for verses that refer to fear, anxiety, peace and comfort. For instance, 1 John 4:18 and Philippians 4:6-9 contain words of wisdom and comfort, especially for someone who is fearful or anxious:

There is no fear in love; but perfect love casteth out fear: because fear hath torment. He that feareth is not made perfect in love. 1 John 4:18

Be careful for nothing; but in everything by prayer and supplication with thanksgiving let your requests be made known unto God. And the peace of God, which passeth all understanding, shall keep your hearts and minds through Christ Jesus. Finally, brethren, whatsoever things are true, whatsoever things are honest, whatsoever things are just, whatsoever things are pure, whatsoever things are lovely, what-soever things are of good report; if there be any virtue, and if there be any praise, think on these things. Those things, which ye have both learned, and received, and heard, and seen in me, do: and the God of peace shall be with you.

Philippians 4:6-9

Apply the strength of the Word recorded in those verses to the model blessing found in Numbers 6:24-26 to create anointed word projectiles for your friend, like this one:

May the Lord God bless you and keep you from all fear and anxiety. May He cause His face to

shine upon you with His power and love, and may He give you a sound mind. Through His perfect love, may God give you grace to cast out fear. May He lift up His countenance upon you with freedom as you tell Him every detail of your need in prayer, and may He give you His peace that surpasses all understanding, as He keeps your heart and mind safe through Jesus Christ.

Paul wrote:

Blessed be God, even the Father of our Lord Jesus Christ, the Father of mercies, and the God of all comfort; who comforteth us in all our tribulation, that we may be able to comfort them which are in any trouble, by the comfort wherewith we ourselves are comforted of God.

2 Corinthians 1:3-4

Your friend struggles with sorrow and grief. You could use a concordance to look for verses that refer to sorrow, grief, peace and comfort. The following anointed word projectiles might be used to intercede for him, if he is experiencing deep sorrow:

May God, the Father of our Lord Jesus Christ, the God of all comfort, encourage your heart and protect you from despair. May He cause His face to shine upon

you as you rejoice in the midst of troubles and trials, putting your faith in Him and being confident of His lovingkindness toward you. May the Lord lift up His countenance upon you with the riches of His joy and pleasure, and may He give you His peace in your heart and soul.

Your friend is walking through a trial. You could use a concordance to look for verses that refer to perseverance and encouragement. The following anointed word projectiles might be used to intercede for him, if he is experiencing an enduring trial. You could use this verse and the definitions of its key words as a basis.

May the God of all grace, who has called you to His eternal glory by Christ Jesus, bless you and keep you strong during this time of testing. May He cause His face to shine upon you and give you grace to endure with patience. May He lift up His countenance upon you to make you perfect and complete in Him, to establish you clearly in the direction He gives you, to strengthen you through spiritual knowledge and by the power of His Holy Spirit as you seek Him with all your heart. May the Lord settle you, making you secure and confident in His love and provision for your peace and well-being.

The Apostle Peter included this blessing in his first letter:

And after you have suffered a little while, the God of all grace [Who imparts all blessing and favor], Who has called you to His [own] eternal glory in Christ Jesus, will Himself complete and make you what you ought to be, establish and ground you securely, and strengthen, and settle you. 1 Peter 5:10, AMPC

As you speak these anointed word projectiles in prayer or speak them directly to the person for whom they are written, you will invoke the power, grace, and blessing of God upon their life.

You could also write out the blessing and mail it or take it to the person for whom you are interceding, and God could use it as a great source of encouragement in their life.

Learn to personalize an anointed word projectile.

CHAPTER 7

RECOGNIZING THE PROPHETIC POWER OF AGREEMENT

Write ye also for the Jews, as it liketh you, in the king's name, and seal it with the king's ring: for the writing which is written in the king's name, and sealed with the king's ring, may no man reverse.

Esther 8:8

Prophetic decree and prophetic proclamation are powerful when used together. In the Bible, royal decrees were followed by the proclamation of those decrees. It was not enough that a king or governor made a decree. That decree had to then be publicized and conveyed throughout the kingdom.

Decree and proclamation were part of a two-step process. Proclamation was the vital announcement of the decree. This allowed people to respond and align themselves to obey the decree.

There is power in public prophetic proclamation, but it also works when it is done in private prayer and intercession. Prophetic proclamations enable God's people to position themselves for and respond to the Father's purposes.

A prophetic decree flows naturally when we comprehend and speak from our heavenly position:

And hath raised us up together, and made us sit together in heavenly places in Christ Jesus.

Ephesians 2:6

The power is not in the words we use, but in the revelation of our authority in Christ.

PROPHETIC DECREES UNLOCK KINGDOM RESOURCES

In the time of Ezra, King Cyrus issued a royal decree to rebuild the Temple at Jerusalem:

But in the first year of Cyrus the king of Babylon the same king Cyrus made a decree to build this house of God. Ezra 5:13

This decree was backed up with royal resources, and the proclamation of that decree unlocked the generous giving and volunteering of those who heard it (see Ezra 1).

King Hezekiah issued a decree inviting Israel and Judah to repent and come to Jerusalem for Passover. That decree resulted in a national revival, as multitudes turned to God, celebrating the Passover for the first time in generations. This was followed by a mass destruction of altars and high places dedicated to false gods (see 2 Chronicles 30 and 31).

In Esther's time, Mordecai wrote a decree in the king's name. This decree mobilized the Jews to overturn the plans of their enemies and brought victory to God's people:

Write ye also for the Jews, as it liketh you, in the king's name, and seal it with the king's ring: for the writing which is written in the king's name, and sealed with the king's ring, may no man reverse.

Esther 8:8

A decree is a royal command. The Aramaic and Hebrew words translated *decree* in these passages could also be translated as judgment, law, commandment, or commission.

According to the *English Dictionary,* the word *law* or *jurisprudence* is "the collection of rules imposed by authority." It is also "a legal document setting forth rules governing a particular kind of activity." In essence, it is a royal edict, an order given by a king or queen. Our royal edict is an order given by King Jesus through the voice of the Holy Spirit, and it has all the weight and authority of the Kingdom of God and the forces of Heaven behind it to carry it out in the Earth realm.

Your prophetic decree also unlocks the resources of the Kingdom. Your words will change atmospheres, touch hearts, break through opposition and shift situations into alignment with God's purposes.

The result of a king's decree was that:

- God's people were positioned to fulfil His purposes.
- The king's treasury was unlocked to resource the decree.
- People responded with generous giving.

- National revival took place, with multitudes turning to God.
- The enemy's plans were over-turned and the enemy was defeated.
- God's people gained victory.
- God's will was accomplished.

HOW TO USE SCRIPTURE AS A PROPHETIC DECREE

Death and life are in the power of the tongue: and they that love it shall eat the fruit thereof.

Proverbs 18:21

What we speak, whether positive or negative, will have consequences. What we declare will bear fruit. James reminds us that our tongues are powerful and that what we speak out of our mouths has power to direct our lives:

Behold, we put bits in the horses' mouths, that they may obey us; and we turn about their whole body. Behold also the ships, which though they be so great, and are driven of fierce winds, yet are they turned about with a very small helm, whithersoever the governor listeth. Even so the tongue is a little member, and boasteth great things. Behold, how great a matter a little fire kindleth! James 3:3-5

The psalmist declared:

For ever, O LORD, thy word is set-tled in heaven. Psalm 119:89

Speaking out scripture can be a powerful way to:

- Strengthen our faith (see Romans 10:17)
- Assist when breakthrough is needed
- Be a weapon in times of spiritual warfare (see Ephesians 6:17).
- Help position us for the fulfillment of God's proposes in our lives.

Learn to recognize the prophetic power of agreement.

CHAPTER 8

TURNING A SCRIPTURE INTO A PROPHETIC DECREE

The Spirit of the LORD is upon me, because he hath anointed me to preach the gospel to the poor; he hath sent me to heal the broken-hearted, to preach deliverance to the captives, and recovering of sight to the blind, to set at liberty them that are bruised, to preach the acceptable year of the LORD.

Luke 4:18-19

A scripture is prophetic when it speaks of the Father's intentions and purposes for our lives. Declaring God's Word is powerful, whether or not it has been given to you through prophetic means or simply because it is divine scripture. Following are some ideas to help you turn a Bible verse into a spoken profession of faith:

- Choose a Bible verse that God has spoken to you or that has prophetic significance to you.
- Choose a scripture you would like to apply by faith to a particular situation you are facing right now or to your overall life and ministry call.

- Personalize the scripture by changing the wording to the first person. You can use the exact wording or adapt it to your own situation as needed.

- Use the present tense because it adds power to your personal declaration.

- Memorize the scripture or write it out and use that to speak from.

Loud, bold declarations are powerful in times of warfare or when breakthrough is needed. However, we do not always need to speak loudly in order for a declaration to be effective. You can speak aloud to yourself, under your breath, or even quietly, and achieve the same results.

EXAMPLES OF SCRIPTURE DECREES FOR ENLARGEMENT

A PROPHETIC DECREE BASED ON JOSHUA 1:

This is a new day. I am entering into the Promised Land. I am entering into the plans and purposes of God for my life. I am entering into my inheritance and receiving God's promises.

Nothing can stand in my way, and no enemy will prevail against me, for God is with me. He will never leave me or forsake me.

I am strong and courageous. I am not fearful or discouraged. I feed on the Word of God. I keep God's Word in my heart, and I obey it. I have success in that which God has called me to.

A PROPHETIC DECREE BASED ON ISAIAH 54:1-5:

I sing. I burst into song, and I shout for joy, for the promises of God are being birthed in my life. The Lord is giving me spiritual children. I am pushing out the boundaries around my life. I am making room. I do not hold back. I am spreading out to the right and the left. My children, both natural and spiritual, will inherit the nations for the Kingdom of God.

I am not afraid, and I do not fear disgrace. I am entering into intimacy with my God, for that is the place where all of these things will be accomplished. God is Almighty, He is my Creator, and He is my Redeemer.

A PROPHETIC DECREE BASED ON LUKE 4:18-19:

The Spirit of the Lord is upon me, because He has anointed me to preach good news to the poor. He has sent me to proclaim freedom for the prisoners and recovery of sight to the blind, to release the oppressed, to proclaim the year of the Lord's favor.

A PROPHETIC DECREE BASED ON 1 CHRONICLES 4:10:

I am blessed, and my territory is enlarged. The hand of the Lord is with me, and I am kept from harm, so that I will be free from pain.

Using these as examples, create your own prophetic decrees in the Spirit.

Learn to turn a scripture into a prophetic decree.

CHAPTER 9

UTILIZING PROPHETIC DECREES

Thou shalt also decree a thing, and it shall be established unto thee: and the light shall shine upon thy ways. When men are cast down, then thou shalt say, There is lifting up; and he shall save the humble person. Job 22:28-29

You will also decree a thing, and it will be established for you; and light will shine on your ways. Job 22:28, NASB

Are you in need of a break-through? A prophetic decree is an authoritative *now* word that unlocks the supernatural and causes a shift to take place.

WHAT IS PROPHETIC DECREE?

A *decree* is "an official order that has the force of law." When we decree something, we are making a declaration that has the weight of Kingdom authority behind it:

Thy kingdom come. Thy will be done in earth, as it is in heaven.
Matthew 6:10

The Kingdom is in you, within you:

102

But if I cast out devils by the Spirit of God, then the kingdom of God is come unto you.   Matthew 12:28

And heal the sick that are therein, and say unto them, The kingdom of God is come nigh unto you. But into whatsoever city ye enter, and they receive you not, go your ways out into the streets of the same, and say, Even the very dust of your city, which cleaveth on us, we do wipe off against you: notwithstanding be ye sure of this, that the kingdom of God is come nigh unto you.

Luke 10:9-11

Our decree is prophetic when it is obtained from our heavenly Father's intention. The Holy Spirit has revealed

God's will to us. We then have authority on Earth to enforce the Father's plans through the agreement of our own words.

When we decree, there is a synchronization in the Spirit. The power of agreement operates in the same time or rate as the mind of God, accomplishing by influencing the course of action of our environment.

A prophetic decree is an expression of Kingdom authority:

Verily I say unto you, Whatsoever ye shall bind on earth shall be bound in heaven: and whatsoever ye shall loose on earth shall be loosed in heaven.

Matthew 18:18

When a king speaks, his subjects must pay attention and obey instantly. As you declare your Father's will through prophetic decree, the spiritual realm must pay attention and come into alignment. Miracles then manifest in the physical realm:

> *And Joshua adjured them at that time, saying, Cursed be the man before the L*ord*, that riseth up and buildeth this city Jericho: he shall lay the foundation thereof in his firstborn, and in his youngest son shall he set up the gates of it.*
>
> Joshua 6:26

This particular prophetic decree was so powerful that it lingered in the atmosphere until all conditions were satisfied. More than five hundred years later it was fulfilled:

In his days did Hiel the Bethelite build Jericho: he laid the foundation thereof in Abiram his firstborn, and set up the gates thereof in his youngest son Segub, according to the word of the Lord, which he spake by Joshua the son of Nun.

1 Kings 16:34

Spoken under the anointing, our prophetic decrees are power-charged with electrifying influence. A prophetic decree flows from the acknowledgement that we are the Father's royal sons and daughters and carry His kingly authority in Jesus' name:

But ye are a chosen generation, a royal priesthood, an holy nation, a peculiar people; that ye should shew forth the praises of him who hath called you out of darkness into his marvellous light.   1 Peter 2:9

And hath made us kings and priests unto God and his Father; to him be glory and dominion for ever and ever. Amen.   Revelation 1:6

It is important to remember that we do not exercise this authority in our own name, but in the name of Jesus:

And whatsoever ye shall ask in my name, that will I do, that the Father may be glorified in the Son.
John 14:13

A prophetic decree is not our own will or wish. It is not a personal desire or what we would like to see happen. It is making a confident declaration of our Father's revealed intention.

God speaks His divine command to you so that you will be His conduit in the Earth realm. You are His agent on Earth, declaring on Earth what your Father has established in Heaven. Your prophetic decree then becomes a powerful and creative "let-there-be" word:

And Jesus answering saith unto them, Have faith in God. For verily I say unto you, That whosoever shall say unto this mountain, Be thou removed, and be thou cast into the sea; and shall not doubt in his heart, but shall believe that those things which he saith shall come to pass; he shall have whatsoever he saith. Mark 11:22-23

Behold, I will make thee a new sharp threshing instrument having teeth: thou shalt thresh the mountains, and beat them small, and shalt make the hills as chaff.

Isaiah 41:15

And he hath made my mouth like a sharp sword; in the shadow of his hand hath he hid me, and made me a polished shaft; in his quiver hath he hid me. Isaiah 49:2

The secret power of a decree is revelation. Revelation spoken from the mouth exposes the truth of a situation.

The essence of it is calling those things which are not as though they were. In other words, it is a prophetic act.

When you speak of something prophetic you are referring to a reality not yet come into existence in the natural Earth realm. A prophetic act, then, is performing an act inspired by the Holy Spirit in the Earth realm to release a powerful shift in the spirit realm. In essence, you release God's truth into the atmosphere.

The action that you perform rises in authority and moves in the power of God to introduce into the atmosphere an action similar to dropping a pebble into a lake. As the pebble is introduced to the water, it disturbs the surface, causing a current that flows outward.

That current begins small, but as it moves outward, it affects a great portion of the lake. And so it is with a prophetic act. It is a small, but significant gesture that moves through the spirit realm, causing a disturbance in the elements, to prepare the natural to receive the supernatural.

Such a prophetic act sends out signals and a pattern to cause the corresponding action to be revealed. It literally sets the precedents and calls into being the will of God for situations and circumstances. Therefore that action is speaking into existence that which does not exist:

(As it is written, I have made thee a father of many nations,) before him whom he believed, even God, who

quickeneth the dead, and calleth those things which be not as though they were. Romans 4:17

Our God gives life to the dead and calls into being what does not yet exist, and we are His instruments in the Earth.

The Bible gives us illustrations of some small prophetic acts that had a great practical impact. In Exodus, for example, we see the hand of Moses against the Amalekites:

And so it was, when Moses held up his hand, that Israel prevailed; and when he let down his hand, Amalek prevailed. But Moses' hands became heavy; so they took a stone and put it under him, and he sat on it. And Aaron and Hur supported his hands, one on one side, and the other on the other side; and his hands were steady until the going down of the sun. So Joshua defeated Amalek and his people with the edge of the sword.

Exodus 17:11-13

It was Moses' prophetic action that released realities in the spirit realm.

Another example, this one with the Prophet Elisha, is found in the book of 2 Kings:

And Elisha said to him, "Take a bow and arrows." So he took a bow and arrows. Then he said to the king of Israel, "Draw the bow," and he drew it. And Elisha laid his hands on the king's hands.

And he said, "Open the window eastward," and he opened it. Then Elisha said, "Shoot," and he shot. And he said, "The LORD's arrow of victory, the arrow of victory over Syria! For you shall fight the Syrians in Aphek until you have made an end of them."

And he said, "Take the arrows," and he took them. And he said to the king of Israel, "Strike the ground with them." And he struck three times and stopped. Then the man of God was angry with him and said, "You should have struck five or six times; then you would have struck down Syria until you had made an end of it, but now you will strike down Syria only three times."

2 Kings 13:15-19, ESV

Some theologians have called this "prophetic intercession." In this type of intercession, the will of God is released on the Earth through the movements or actions of a believer as they are directed by God. The actions or movements of the Earth realm then release a specific blessing or reality in the spirit realm.

Prophetic acts were not uncommon in Bible times. Actions that changed destinies were released as well as words. Because God is multifaceted, He did not confine Himself to words alone. Through acts and movements, the prophetic can control, influence and remove restrictions preventing the reality of the spirit realm from manifesting in the natural realm.

Prophetic acts were the primary method of prophetic ministry for the Old Testament prophet Ezekiel. Many of his messages were made understandable through the prophetic acts he performed.

For example, Ezekiel used his hair as part of a prophetic act:

And thou, son of man, take thee a sharp knife, take thee a barber's razor, and cause it to pass upon thine head and upon thy beard: then take thee balances to weigh, and divide the hair. Thou shalt burn with fire a third part in the midst of the city, when the days of the siege are fulfilled: and thou shalt take a third part, and smite about it with a knife: and a third part thou shalt scatter in the wind; and I will draw out a sword after them. Thou shalt also take thereof a few in number, and bind them in thy skirts. Then take of them again, and cast them into the midst of the fire, and burn them in the fire; for thereof shall a fire come forth into all the house of Israel. Ezekiel 5:1-4

In the New Testament, the prophet Agabus performed a prophetic act with Paul's belt to deliver the Word of the Lord to Paul:

And as we tarried there many days, there came down from Judaea a certain prophet, named Agabus. And when he was come unto us, he took Paul's girdle, and bound his own hands and feet, and said, Thus saith the Holy Ghost, So shall the Jews at Jerusalem bind the man that owneth this girdle, and shall deliver him into the hands of the Gentiles. Acts 21:10-11

Being sensitive to God's voice and to His instructions to the exact precise detail will bring great victory. We should ask God daily to gives us creativity in our thought life so we can provide the prophetic acts to bring His will into the earth realm.

God designed us to be able to defend ourselves and to defeat the strategies of the enemy without having to use external weapons. Again the greatest tool we have, our greatest weapon, is our mouth:

> *And he hath made my mouth like a sharp sword; in the shadow of his hand hath he hid me, and made me a polished shaft; in his quiver hath he hid me.*   Isaiah 49:2

The word *mouth* in the Hebrew denotes "sound, speech, and two-edged word." *Hand* indicates "power and dominion." *A polished shaft* meant a choice arrow which, being polished with oil, was able to pierce deeper.

God has given your anointed words the ability to be used as a two-edged sword with the leverage to dominate, under the shadow of His authority. He anoints you with influence so you might be effective in every sphere. You have the power to not only affect the spirit realm, but also the natural realm—emotionally, physically and mentally.

God's greatest plan can be activated by mere words. When under attack, we don't have to grope around, looking for a weapon. We are the weapon. We have the ammunition resident in our spirit, namely, the Word of God. Jesus said, *"I come in the volume of the book"*:

Then said I, Lo, I come (in the volume of the book it is written of me,) to do thy will, O God.

Hebrews 10:7

All truth is parallel. When we have a revelation of God's Word for a situation, that qualifies us to come in the volume of the book. You don't have to be a scholar in the Word. You only have to know what the will of the Lord is for any given situation.

Learn to utilize prophetic decrees.

CHAPTER 10

UNDERSTANDING THE ANATOMY OF A BLESSING

Therefore God give thee of the dew of heaven, and the fatness of the earth, and plenty of corn and wine: let people serve thee, and nations bow down to thee: be lord over thy brethren, and let thy mother's sons bow down to thee: cursed be every one that curseth thee, and blessed be he that blesseth thee.

Genesis 27:28-29

There are certain actions and attitudes which combine to make the biblical tool known as a blessing uniquely effective. A blessing, as described in the Scriptures, always included five elements:

1. A meaningful and appropriate touch
2. A spoken message
3. Attaching high value to the one being blessed
4. Picturing a special future for him or her
5. An active commitment to fulfill the blessing

Let's review each of these elements in greater detail:

MEANINGFUL TOUCH

Meaningful touch was an essential element in bestowing a blessing in Old Testament times. Isaac gave us a picture of this action when he called his son to come near and kiss him. This produced a physical connection to him:

> *And his father Isaac said unto him* [Jacob], *Come near now, and kiss me, my son.*   Genesis 27:26

This incident was not an isolated one. Each time a blessing was given in the Scriptures, a meaningful touch provided a caring background to the words that would be spoken. Kissing, hugging or the laying on of hands were all part of bestowing a blessing.

A meaningful touch has many beneficial effects. The act of touching is key to communicating warmth, personal acceptance, affirmation, and even physical health. For any person who wishes to bless a child, touch must be an integral part of that blessing.

A SPOKEN MESSAGE

The second element of the blessing involves a spoken message, one that is actually put into words. In many homes today, such words of love and acceptance are seldom received. Parents sometimes assume that simply being present communicates a blessing, but a blessing fulfills its purpose only when it is actually verbalized—spoken in person, written down or, preferably, both.

Abraham spoke a blessing to his son Isaac. Isaac spoke a blessing to his son Jacob. Jacob gave a verbal blessing to each of his twelve sons and to two of his grandchildren.

When God blessed us with the gift of His Son, it was His Word that *"became flesh and dwelt among us"*:

And the Word was made flesh, and dwelt among us, (and we beheld his glory, the glory as of the only begotten of the Father,) full of grace and truth.　　　John 1:14

God has always been a God of words, and we must be a people of words.

ATTACHING HIGH VALUE TO THE
ONE BEING BLESSED

To convey a blessing, the words must attach high value to the person being blessed. In blessing Jacob, Isaac said, *"Surely, the smell of my son is like the smell of a field which the Lord has blessed. ... Let peoples serve you, and nations bow down to you:*

> *And he came near, and kissed him: and he smelled the smell of his raiment, and blessed him, and said, See, the smell of my son is as the smell of a field which the LORD hath blessed.*
> *Let people serve thee, and nations bow down to thee: be lord over thy brethren, and let thy mother's sons*

bow down to thee: cursed be every one that curseth thee, and blessed be he that blesseth thee.

Genesis 27:27 and 29

Jacob had to be a very valuable person to merit having nations bow down to him. Calling him *"a blessed field"* was implying that he was like a field where there was tremendous growth and life.

In this way, Isaac used a word picture, that of a field, to describe how valuable his son was to him. Word pictures are a powerful way of communicating acceptance.

PICTURING A SPECIAL FUTURE

A fourth element of a blessing is the way it pictures a special future for the person being blessed. Isaac said to his son Jacob, *"May God give you of the dew of heaven, of the fatness of the earth. ... Let peoples serve you, and nations bow down to you"*:

> *Therefore God give thee of the dew of heaven, and the fatness of the earth, and plenty of corn and wine: let people serve thee, and nations bow down to thee: be lord over thy brethren, and let thy mother's sons bow down to thee: cursed be every one that curseth thee, and blessed be he that blesseth thee.*
>
> Genesis 27:28-29

Even today, Jewish homes are noted for picturing a special future for their children. One story I heard illustrates this activity well. Jewish mothers are known to introduce their children, not only by their name, but also including the profession the parents expect them to excel in in the future. A young Jewish mother, when asked, "What are your children names?" might reply, pointing to each child in turn, "This is Bennie, the doctor, and Reuben, the lawyer."

Isaac believed his sons had great potential and a special future before them. He communicated that belief in his blessing, just as we should communicate a future hope to those we seek to bless.

Because of the unique position we have in Christ, our words carry with them the weight of God's intended purpose. When we pronounce a blessing, we help those we are blessing see a future that is full of life and opportunity. We are letting them know that we believe they can build an outstanding life and future with the strength and ability God has given them.

AN ACTIVE COMMITMENT

The last element of a blessing concerns the responsibility that goes with giving that blessing. For the patriarchs, God Himself stood behind the blessing they bestowed on their children. And, in the same way, parents today need to rely on the Lord to bring the words of their blessing to fruition.

Words alone cannot communicate a blessing. These words must be backed up by our willingness to do everything possible to help the one being blessed to become successful. For instance, you can tell your son that he has the talent to be a very good drummer, but then if you don't provide a drum set for him to practice on, how can her perfect his gift. If you fail to make opportunities available to those you bless, your lack of commitment will actually under-mine your blessing.

Be creative in blessing. Maintain an appropriate physical touch, speak the message God has given you. Speak positive statements, using word pic-tures. And then do what you can to equip the individual.

Learn to understand the anatomy of a blessing.

CHAPTER 11

BECOMING FAMILIAR WITH SCRIPTURAL BLESSINGS

Freely ye have received, freely give.

Matthew 10:8

TRUST THE LORD TO GUIDE YOU

As you make yourself available to intercede for others with anointed word projectiles, the Lord will open your spiritual eyes and ears to comprehend what He wants to accomplish in the lives of those individuals. Be careful not to enforce *your* desire on them because that would be interpreted as white witchcraft. *White witchcraft* is defined as "superimposing your will on another." Any form of control or manipulation falls under the category of witchcraft.

Offer God's anointed word projectiles from His Word to others. Then put your confidence in God to carry out His Word according to His will and His timing.

Jesus instructed His disciples to minister to others in the power of the Holy Spirit, according to the grace given unto them. The rest was up to God.

The following New Testament passages are appropriate for use in spoken blessings:

- Romans 15:5-6 and 13
- 1 Corinthians 1:4-9 and 16:23
- 2 Corinthians 1:3-7, 2:14 and 13:7-9
- Ephesians 1:3-23, 3:14-21, 6:18-20 and 23-24
- Philippians 1:3-6, 9-11; 4:6-8 and 23
- Colossians 1:3-6, 9-14 and 4:2-6
- 1 Thessalonians 1:2-3, 3:12-13, 5:23-24 and 28
- 2 Thessalonians 1:11-12, 2:16-17 and 3:5-16
- 2 Timothy 4:22
- Philemon 1:4-7
- Hebrews 13:20-21
- 1 Peter 1:3-9 and 5:10-11
- 2 Peter 1:2-4 and 3:18
- 2 John 1:3
- 2 John 1:2-3

Interceding for others with anointed word projectiles is one way you can freely give to others in Jesus's name. [1]

Familiarize yourself with scriptural blessings.

1. Adapted from *The Power of Spoken Blessings* by Bill Gothard,published 2004 by Multnomah Books, Colorado Springs, Colorado.

CHAPTER 12

PRONOUNCING BLESSINGS

*Behold, I have received command-
ment to bless: and he hath blessed;
and I cannot reverse it.*

Numbers 23:20

Genesis 48:8-20 gives us insight
into how to pronounce blessings.
The time had come for the patri-
arch Jacob to die, which meant that
the time of the blessing upon his
children and grandchildren was
to begin. Now one hundred and

forty-seven years old, Jacob began the process of blessing his sons, and he began by blessing the sons of Joseph.

The Israeli custom was for a man to lay his hands upon his children and pass down a blessing to them. He could lay his left hand upon any and all of his children and prophesy promises over them. But his right hand was placed on one son only. This blessing was normally reserved for the firstborn son, because custom dictated that he be the legal heir of the family inheritance.

Earlier Jacob had cheated his older brother Esau out of the blessing, and the right-hand blessing was so powerful that once it was given, it was considered irreversible:

Behold, I have received command-
ment to bless: and he hath blessed;
and I cannot reverse it.

Numbers 23:20

Isaac answered, "Your brother
tricked me and stole your blessing.
Esau replied, "My brother deserves
the name Jacob, because he has
already cheated me twice. The first
time he cheated me out of my rights
as the first-born son, and now he
has cheated me out of my blessing."
Then Esau asked his father, "Don't
you still have any blessing left for
me?"
"My son," Isaac answered, "I have
made Jacob the ruler over you and
your brothers, and all of you will be
his servants. I have also promised

him all the grain and grapes that he needs. There's nothing left that I can do for you."

"Father," Esau asked, "don't you have more than one blessing? You can surely give me a blessing too!" Then Esau started crying again.

Genesis 27:35-38, CEV

Once a blessing was pronounced, it went into the future of the recipient and began the process of shaping God's redemptive destiny for that person.

In another place in the Bible, Joseph brought his two sons, Manasseh and Ephraim, to his father so that they might receive a blessing. Since Manasseh was the oldest, Joseph desired for him to receive the best of his father's blessings, so he guided him toward Jacob's right hand:

And Joseph took them both, Ephraim in his right hand toward Israel's left hand, and Manasseh in his left hand toward Israel's right hand, and brought them near unto him.   Genesis 48:13

When the boys stood in front of Jacob, the text says that he guided his hands *"wittingly,"* meaning that he placed them that way on purpose. He crossed his arms, laying his right hand on the youngest boy, Ephraim, and the other hand on Manasseh:

And Israel stretched out his right hand, and laid it upon Ephraim's head, who was the younger, and his left hand upon Manasseh's head, guiding his hands wittingly; for Manasseh was the firstborn.

Genesis 48:14

This word *wittingly* in the Hebrew denotes "to act circumspectly, intelligent, with wisdom and understanding." There can be no doubt that Jacob acted with intent.

RIGHT- AND LEFT-HAND BLESSINGS

Joseph saw the apparent mistake of his father, and thinking that it was done due to Jacob's inability to see properly, he grabbed his father's hands and tried to uncross them:

And when Joseph saw that his father laid his right hand upon the head of Ephraim, it displeased him: and he held up his father's hand, to remove it from Ephraim's head unto Manasseh's head. And Joseph said unto his father, Not so, my father: for this is the firstborn; put thy right hand upon his head.

Genesis 48:17-18

Jacob was well aware of what he had done and he proceeded to explain to Joseph that while the eldest son would be great, the younger one would be even greater.

This entire scenario is a shadow of God crossing His hands to bless the gentiles. Israel is God's firstborn, but God chose to bless other nations through Christ:

And thou shalt say unto Pharaoh, Thus saith the LORD, Israel is my son, even my firstborn.   Exodus 4:22

Today, the membership of the Church of Jesus Christ is comprised predominately of gentiles, the second choice of the Gospel:

Then Paul and Barnabas waxed bold, and said, It was necessary that the word of God should first have been spoken to you [the Jews]: *but seeing ye put it from you, and judge yourselves unworthy of everlasting life, lo, we turn to the Gentiles.*

Acts 13:46

For the most part, Israel rejected the Gospel message, so God turned His

144

love and favor toward all who would accept His Son Jesus. Jesus prophesied that the first would be last and the last would be first, meaning that Israel was first called but will be the last saved, while the Gentiles were the last called but the first saved:

> *But many that are first shall be last; and the last shall be first.*
>   Matthew 19:30

According to Jewish custom, the firstborn son was the deserving one for all legal rights and privileges. His siblings were considered blessed, but the elder received the dominant blessing. God saw the firstborn, who were His chosen Jewish people, and crossed His hands for us, offering salvation and redemption to the less deserving, gentile world. Because God crossed His hands at the cross, you and I are blessed with the right-hand blessing, God's best blessing.

There may be those who are better qualified, but God crossed His arms and choose you for the position. There may be those who have a better health condition, but God gives you productivity in your condition until healing manifests in your body. There may be those who have a better financial score, but God will repair your credit. There may be those who have a better income, but as you tithe, He will bless you to have more than enough left over, so that you can finance His Kingdom. There may be those who have a better credit history, but God will give you extended favor so that your loans will be approved. There may be those who have a better education, but you will be chosen because of your experience. There may be those who have a better job performance, but God will raise you up and cause those in charge to choose you over others.

The dominant blessing of God brings a radical change to your spiritual geographies. There is a horizontal shift in your spiritual landscape that affects your life and the life of all those connected to you:

And he answered and spake unto those that stood before him, saying, Take away the filthy garments from him. And unto him he said, Behold,

BALLISTIC APOSTOLIC PRAYER

I have caused thine iniquity to pass from thee, and I will clothe thee with change of raiment.

Zechariah 3:4

The word *raiment* in Hebrew is *makh-al-aw-tsaw'*, which denotes "a mantle." The main idea is that of "a covering such as a cloak or other article of clothing." In biblical times, a mantle was typically a large, loosely fitting garment made of animal skin.

In First Kings, we see an image of the concept of a cloak:

So he departed thence, and found Elisha the son of Shaphat, who was plowing with twelve yoke of oxen before him, and he with the twelfth: and Elijah passed by him, and cast his mantle upon him. 1 Kings 19:19

The prophet Elijah threw his cloak around Elisha as a symbol of his ministry being passed on to Elisha. This mantle was the official garment of a prophet. It automatically marked a man as a prophet, a spokesman for God. It represented the call of God and the protection of the Holy Spirit on that call.

God caused our faults and our mischiefs to pass from us and clothed us with a change of attitude and expectation. Once that change takes place, the blessing of God covers our life like a cloak. It is as if we are wrapped in protection, concealed from the sight of the adversary, to avoid major attacks, and enveloped with supernatural favor. That mantle provides us authority and responsibility as God's chosen elect.

There are many clearly many ways to pronounce a blessing. Let us learn to do it with power and wisdom.

CHAPTER 13

SOME CONCLUDING THOUGHTS

For the word of God is living and active, and sharper than any two-edged sword, penetrating even as far as the division of soul and spirit, and of joints and marrows, and able to judge the thoughts and intentions of the heart.

Hebrews 4:12, BSB

What a powerful weapon you have in your tongue! Now, it's your choice:

- Will you use your tongue for blessing or for cursing?
- Will you choose life or death?
- Will you become an instrument of healing and deliverance for those around you or will you only add to the chaos and confusion of our time?
- Will you live and allow others to live under the curse of the enemy or will you pick up your spiritual mantle of authority and become a conqueror and a deliverer?

I trust that you will make the right choice today.

If you have enjoyed these books on intercessory prayer and spiritual warfare, please look for coming editions that will continue to expand our understanding of these all-important subjects.

Other Books
by
Prophetess Jackie Harewood

Sing Unto the Lord a New Song: An Introduction to Praise and Worship
(0-97-9712623-0-6)

The Violent Take It by Force
(978-1-934769-11-9)

Intercession Builds Bridges: Frequently Asked Questions About Intercession
(978-1-59872-909-2)

Overshadowed by the Almighty
(978-1-934769-99-7)

Ballistic Apostolic Prayer
(978-1-940461-55-7)

The Violent Take it by Force

Force

Intercession Made Easy

Jackie Harewood

Overshadowed
by the Almighty

Understanding
the Phenomeno
Known as
"Being Slain
in the Spirit"

With a special
chapter entitled
What Does God's Voice
Sound Like?

Prophetess Jackie Harewood

Ballistic Apostolic Prayer

Jackie Harewood

I *Will* Bless THEE

Discovering
the
Untapped
Power of
COVENANT

Apostle David Harewood

AUTHOR CONTACT PAGE

Prophetess Jackie Harewood
37041 Agnes Webb Avenue
Prairieville, LA 70769

jharewoodla@cox.net
(225) 772-14552

www.ingramcontent.com/pod-product-compliance
Lightning Source LLC
LaVergne TN
LVHW092324080426
835508LV00039B/526